THE YORKSHIRE MOORS AND WOLDS

Mark Denton

THE YORKSHIRE
MOORS AND WOLDS

Mark Denton

F

FRANCES LINCOLN LIMITED
PUBLISHERS

Frances Lincoln Ltd
4 Torriano Mews
Torriano Avenue
London NW5 2RZ
www.franceslincoln.com

British Library Cataloguing-in-Publication data
A catalogue record for this book is available from the British Library.

ISBN 978-0-7112-2824-5

Printed and bound in Singapore

9 8 7 6 5 4 3 2 1

above
Lake, Londesborough Park

half title page
Rainbow over Littlebeck

title page
Square bales, Londesborough Wold

**In memory of my grandmother,
Mary Bell Storey,
who took me to Filey**

CONTENTS

FOREWORD

This book traces my panoramic photography right back to the start. Even before I began photographing the Yorkshire coast, I used to take walks out across the Wolds from my former home in Hunmanby. The camera would go on my back in an impossibly small and undesirably cheap rucksack, and a similarly inexpensive tripod, the type that might fall over in a light breeze, was slung over my right shoulder. Since then, the kit may have become more expensive (and considerably heavier), but the principles for seeking out images seem to have barely changed at all, with constant references to my viewfinder, wondering whether I look more like David Bailey or Inspector Clouseau.

The very first successful image from my panoramic camera appears here on pages 82–3: a sunset in July, looking north across the fields and up the hill, just fifty yards from my front door. The shot was one of the first to appear on my embryonic website, where I cheated and scanned the transparency the wrong way round, putting the silhouetted trees on the left where I thought they looked more effective. Here I have restored them to their natural position on the right of the image; I feel no urge to cheat these days.

Moors and Wolds? This may seem an unusual subject for a book. They are two quite different landscapes, separated by the wide gulf of the Vale of Pickering. I could have comfortably ignored the Wolds, as most people do. But the Wolds are my back yard, a place any landscape photographer will have explored and developed an affection for. Moreover, the Yorkshire Wolds are a stunning tract of countryside in themselves, unique to England and just about unique *in* England. So the surprise should be that so few have taken time to photograph them before, rather than that someone now does. This book presents the vast variety of conditions and landscapes within just a relatively small section of the British Isles, something that a pinhead would cover on a map of the world. Where else do you find such beauty combined with the variety in a country of similar size to Britain? New Zealand possibly: but where else? Half of us seem to spend our lives planning our escape. In terms of nature on our doorstep we really don't know how lucky we are.

Lost on the Wolds

The Yorkshire Wolds are reputed to be the least visited place in England. True or not, that's one reason why I like them. Unlike the Lake District, there are few awkward vehicular meetings on country roads and, unlike the Dales, few pedestrians to nod to on the pathways. Call me anti-social, but it's rather nice to go about my business undisturbed sometimes. The thought that someone watching me is thinking 'What on earth is he up to?' often haunts me on my shoots, not least because I'm often wondering the same thing myself!

Such is the solitude on the Wolds that it comes as a shock to run into anyone at all; it's just so unexpected. One winter morning near Staxton, I dragged myself out of a ditch and literally through a hedgerow, to face a shocked woman walking her dog. All I could offer was a beaming 'lovely morning', as is the British way. If in doubt, refer to the weather. The look on her face was priceless, as if I were an escaped lunatic, although if she did call the police, they weren't quite quick enough to intercept me.

The Wolds are empty not just of tourists, but of people generally. When I stumbled across a recently departed calf, my over-active social consciousness kicked in and I felt an urgent need to inform somebody. I traversed another four miles before finding a farm, and even then no one was visible. I eventually found a neighbour who promised to tell 'someone', but I wasn't entirely convinced there was anyone to tell. This ten-mile circle from my former home in Hunmanby was negotiated four times, all in bright sunshine and on well-marked 'popular' pathways. I never did meet anyone coming the other way.

When driving, the only regular vehicles are the four-wheel drives of the custodians of this green and pleasant land. When they see me, I'm sure they assume I'm lost. If lost means that I don't necessarily care which particular road I'm on they'd usually be right. The Romans did build the occasional straight over the hills here, but the other roads typically meander without any good reason, often without signposts. I will usually return home and consult the map to see where I've been (a nonsensical reverse of logic) and discover that the route that got me from place A to place B could have been achieved in a fraction of the time if I'd turned in entirely the opposite direction at place C. I fear for any uninitiated tourist that turns off the A166 on the way to the coast; there's probably an undiscovered dale with hundreds of rusting vehicles a few miles off the main road. Nevertheless, my extra miles are rarely wasted as new vistas come into view, or forgotten places are refreshed in memory.

Encounters with other humans are so rare that almost all become committed to memory. I still wonder who the men were in the mysterious dark vans I saw during the winter, and why I passed ten black SUVs in succession on the road to Thixendale. The sound of gunfire permeates the air a various times of year, adding to my general sense of nervous paranoia. Needless to say, I've yet to meet anyone carrying a gun; outside of the villages and most popular walks, I've yet to meet anyone on foot at all.

Despite the lack of inhabitants, the Wolds are intensively farmed. Field patchworks characterise much of this land, with breaks for steep-sided chalk valleys where sheep and cattle roam. This is an agricultural landscape, in which tractor drivers must fully earn their corn; there are few bowling greens in this part of East Yorkshire. I always imagine the shape of the hills as bread cakes rising in an oven: a child's picture of hills, 'Teletubby' hills even, if like me you have a toddler about the house. Lumps of chalk are visible scattered across the surface of the fields from autumn to spring, to the extent that in some places it appears from a distance that crops must grow straight from solid rock. The only comparable landscape I've found is in the Purbeck Hills of Dorset, curiously formed from the very same band of chalk that rises at Flamborough, dips, and then resurfaces hundreds of miles away on the south coast. It's a quintessentially English landscape and yet almost entirely hidden from the view.

In some ways, I feel I've yet to capture the true essence of these hills on film. Although they undulate beautifully, there are few genuine vantage points (though I'm sure there are some even now that I've yet to find). My best tactic is to pick out landscape features and of course to look to the sky, as the Wolds seem to provide a perfect balance for photography between air and earth as the lack of tree cover usually allows an easy sightline to a distant horizon. I'll keep looking for that definitive Wolds image, and I'll let you know how I get on. If I can find my way home.

Over the Moors

I first came to the North Yorkshire Moors as a child, or rather was bussed over them *en route* from my native Sunderland to Butlin's in Filey. Holidays had to be relatively inexpensive, but if you'd given me a choice between Filey and Corfu, I'm sure I would have chosen Filey gladly. If the journey didn't exactly become familiar (I made the trip with my grandmother three times if I remember correctly), particular features stuck in the memory. The hill near Scaling Dam is neither as steep nor as tall as childhood imagination made it, but still brings reminiscences. The early warning 'golf balls' of Fylingdales, visible in those days from the A171, were a sight that caused a young lad much excitement, not least because it meant we were shortly to arrive in Filey.

The Moors of my imagination were bathed in permanent sunshine, and perhaps this is not too unrealistic as our trips during Whit week usually coincided with good weather. I had little concept of the harsh weather that can dominate the open moorland other than a tale of relatives stranded in Whitby for an extra day by the snow. The experience of childhood now can't help but seem a little unreal. Perhaps the more you revisit, the more places are updated in memory, sometimes without the golden sunshine of youth. Or possibly going back to a place years later actually hinders the memory, springs a surprise or plays tricks. What I thought was my first ever visit to Nunnington in the Howardian Hills produced an extraordinary sense of *déjà vu*, though quite what combination of day tripping or mystery touring produced the source of these memories completely escapes me. And it can only be speculated what the ten-year-old boy would have made of living in Hunmanby, just a couple of miles inland from Filey and site of a model railway that was a favourite day trip. In reality, when I first returned to Filey, the Butlin's site was a flat wasteland interspersed with the occasional pile of rubble. The Gaiety Theatre, rows of chalets and swimming pool were a distant memory.

So for many years after these childhood excursions, the North Yorkshire Moors passed me by, in a literal sense through the windows of cars, trains and buses. I would only see the outer edge of the Cleveland Hills from the A19 or the east coast mainline, though in reality any real interest in what went on there was yet to germinate. Typically, as an older teenager there were far more important issues to be dealt with, and the most important issue on any trip or holiday would be the consumption of alcohol. Only during my degree years did the urge to explore Britain start to grow, with a first trip to the Lake District since a tedious school trip to Ullswater.

One memory from those student years still sticks in the mind. I spent one year studying (a dubious description of what I was doing there) in Middlesbrough, and for one lecture had to scale the large university tower block in the centre of town. For some reason I was early – I must have thought that if I was actually going to attend a lecture I may as well be prompt. What the lecture was about I can't recall, but I can certainly remember the view. Here was the incredible juxtaposition of Teesside and North Yorkshire; out of one side of the building the largest industrial site in Western Europe, and the other the apparently endless Moors, of which the curious pinnacle of Roseberry Topping signalled the beginning. This was far from a 'road to Damascus' moment, my hangover and general outlook on life would have precluded that, but I think it must have made a great impression on the subconscious, as I have never forgotten that moment.

Falling for Falling Foss

Having obtained my first panoramic camera in the summer of 2003, I curiously spent a couple of months doing what could best be described as dithering. Of course I used the camera when I initially received it, as much to check that it was functioning correctly as anything else. But after a few local walks, a short trip to the Lakes and a couple of days on the coast, it went back into the bag for a number of weeks. In my defence, I was busy updating the rest of my equipment. The finest of cameras also demanded the best in filtration and light metering, as film could be quite an expensive commodity just to waste. However, I was guilty of waiting for inspiration to arrive on my doorstep rather than making the effort to hunt it down. Finally an urge that became very familiar in the ensuing months must have grabbed me and I went searching for panoramas.

The autumn helped in breaking me out of my indolence. I was, of course, a great admirer of Joe Cornish's images and on more than one occasion bought his greetings card of May Beck as it tumbles into a tranquil pool near to the waterfall of Falling Foss. The shot was classic Cornish: a jubilant celebration of autumn from the detailed foreground leaves to the glorious wild colour of the framing trees. I had visited the Foss before, but it was in early summer and the colours had been flat and dominated by green.

Supported by a length of rope (not entirely essential, but I'm cautious by nature), I half-slid, half-sidled down the slope to Littlebeck, as May Beck becomes known after the leap over Falling Foss. After a damp scramble upstream along the beck I emerged into the mini amphitheatre formed at the base of the falls and began my shoot. It was really my first targeted expedition to shoot a specific subject: something that would become my *modus operandi* in the months to follow.

The results were tainted by inexperience and by my desire to experiment in a less than methodical fashion. This was early November and few autumnal leaves actually remained on the trees, but I became overly distracted by the notion that I should use what remained. Of the images I produced most were spoilt by these leaves covering one side of the image or the other. Not only were they ugly and too sparse, covering the slide like strands of hair inadequately covering a bald head, they were also moving in the breeze, a fact that I'd essentially overlooked, and an important one given that exposures are rarely less than a second in woodland and often significantly more. The combination was far from appealing. At the time, I was feeling rather smug after all this clever composing, and felt sure that I had something good in the can. Something must have told me that I ought to have some sort of souvenir of my outing, and I decided to finish off with a rather boring image of Falling Foss defined by its setting. I moved back towards the walls of the ravine to allow the panoramic format to make the most of its near 90-degree coverage and shot an image with the falls on the left and a tree on the right. Naturally this is the image that makes an appearance in this book (page 54). Although hardly prize-winning, in stark contrast to the other shots from the session, it was simplistic and well balanced and effectively told the story of that part of the world at that particular moment. The glorious carpet of golden leaves also helped, but I'll have to let Mother Nature take the credit for that.

It was a surprise when the slides were returned from the lab, and there continue to be surprises to this day. Fortunately a greater proportion are now of the pleasant variety, but it was very good to learn some of these lessons early on. It told me immediately that composition in my chosen format would be far from an easy artform, but on the positive side that effective panoramas could be achieved in relatively intimate surroundings without resorting to wacky focussing or angles, and not just from the tops of large hills.

Thus began an extended love affair with Falling Foss and May Beck, so much so that I needed the images to explain to my better half where I'd been! I returned three times in the following week alone and only gave up when storms had ripped the final leaves from the trees and the golden carpet had been reduced to a rotting brown mush. That week and the following year produced so many images that I almost felt that I'd exhausted every element of the potential of the location, but I'm sure I'm mistaken. Give it a little time and I will return, and I'm sure it will seem as fresh as that first muddy adventure of my photographic career.

The Trouble with Sheep

I consider myself a friend of the countryside. I'm not a tub-thumping green campaigner, but I'm certainly 'eco-aware', if a little fatalistic about what we can actually do about global warming and the other issues on the table. On my walks I will religiously close gates and pick up the tiniest scrap of litter that might have fallen from my bag. All in all, I just love being out there – breathing in the air, absorbing the atmosphere. I also have a great love of the wildlife and livestock that a regularly run into. When alone (I must stress that) I will regularly chat to any cows, sheep, horses and the like that I see on my walk. When I say 'chat to', the conversations rarely go past the stage of a cheery greeting or 'How are you?' but they do pass the time and amuse me. Sadly my pleasantries are rarely acknowledged, but thus far this is yet to discourage me to any great extent. Recently however, I have begun to wonder if the animals are beginning to resent my constant interruptions to their idyllic peace and have formed an action committee in order to address the problem.

You don't expect much trouble from sheep. Engrossed in a dawn shoot at Red Scarth Woods (see pages 24–5), I looked up from my viewfinder to find my lofty perch entirely encircled by rather irate examples of the species, the type with horns. I was forced to abandon my position using the tripod to point an escape route and can count myself lucky that the best conditions had been and gone before the offensive.

My most memorable sheep encounter, however, came in an entirely different set of circumstances. It was an ugly October day of glowering grey skies, with intermittent rain bouncing off my waterproof and walking boots caked in wet mud. I left the road at the Flask Inn at Fylingdales at a small dene I wanted to explore named Biller Howe Dale. I liked what I found there, and the trees afforded a degree of shelter from any rain, but one of my faults surfaced and I began to think the grass was greener (or in this case the leaves more golden) on the other side of the fence. I'd noted on the map that my favourite destination on the Moors, May Beck, was not too far away, and I made for the horizon across the open moorland known as Biller Howe Dale Slack. A broken green line clearly marked the course, on paper, if not on the ground. Finding what I thought was a path through the heather I confidently strode on, though it wasn't long before doubts surfaced. In retrospect, I probably wasn't following a path at all, more likely a sheep trail. It appeared to be running in a straight line, though I would guess that sheep sometimes like to travel in straight lines too. The sodden path soon began to peter out and be replaced by an indecipherable maze of vivid green bog and black heather. 'Right', I said to myself, 'I'm not going to quit. I'm just going to walk straight over it. After all, I can see my destination on the horizon'.

My left leg sank in to the ankle. Worse was to follow as my right plunged straight in, up to the knee, and carried on sinking. A thousand docu-drama emergencies ran through my head in a flash of panic, each with a grave Michael Buerk voiceover soundtrack. 'The walker quickly sank in as far as his neck, with the nearest help over three miles away.' Instinctively I fell onto my back in order to spread my weight, and then rolled to my right to use the twisting motion to dislodge the trapped leg from the swamp. It emerged with a hearty sucking noise, the sort that comes from plunging a large spoon into blancmange, and I lay there relieved for just a moment.

Just about long enough to realise I'd rolled next to the carcass of a sheep; rib cage standing proud of the swamp with bleached and matted wool still clinging to the bones, and a terrifying skull, level with my head, appearing to laugh at me. I could hardly blame it. I'd not experienced such ignominy since I fell in the pool below Hardraw Force. It was about at this point that I decided I had a clear choice: to perish in Hardeysque fashion on the Moor and have my body quietly subsumed by nature and never found, or give up. So, ten seconds later and about thirty seconds after I had promised myself there would be no way I would give in, I was busy quitting, and if I'm honest having a good laugh at the melodrama of it all. I think it unlikely that there was anyone around to hear the brief scream I let out as my eyes met those of the skull, and it's even less likely that anyone will find out about it now.

I played out the afternoon with an enjoyable, stress-free shoot in Biller Howe Dale. Even the sun came out late on, as if to compliment me on my decision. Then again, life would be so much duller without the odd madcap decision. It won't be the last.

Sunset at Roseberry Topping.

Late June at Roseberry, and the sun declines to the north-west over Middlesborough. The vivid side-lighting unveils various pits and scars on the hillside, a reminder that the shape of the iconic landmark owes a great deal to the quarrying and earthworking.

Late sun, Roseberry Topping

Breaking cloud, Roseberry Topping

The path to the Topping, Newton Wood

The Cleveland Hills in May

Shifting patterns in the season make the optimum time to visit Roseberry and Newton Wood a moveable feast, but the meeting of bluebells and fields of oilseed rape in May should not be missed. The small crest of Cliff Ridge provides a fabulous panoramic view both to the north over the Topping and to the south to the edge of the Moors.

Pathway, Newton Wood

Bluebells, Newton Wood

Setting sun at Sutton Bank

The flat expanse of the Vale of York darkens as the sun sets in February. When visiblity is good the rising ground of the Yorkshire Dales is clear to the south and east.

White Horse of Kilburn

Cleveland Way signpost, Whitestonecliff

Whorl Hill view at dawn, near Swainby

The view from Scarth Wood Moor is a firm favourite among landscape photographers, and it's easy to see why. For this delightful February dawn, I was joined by a large circle of unappreciative sheep. Thankfully they allowed me time to capture such details as a more docile circle of cows in the foreground and the tiny pinnacle of Roseberry Topping in the far distance.

Clearing mist, Easterside, Ryedale

Easterside Farm at dawn, near Hawnby

Horses, Helmsley Castle

We arrived in Hawnby in July 2005, shortly after flash floods had destroyed bridges and threatened lives on the River Rye.

I was already aware of the storms, having driven through them with a friend on the A170. The huge tempest was visible from the road covering the entire Vale of Pickering and giving lightning that appeared constant, as if someone was flicking a light switch. We stopped at the turn-off to Whitby to attempt to shoot it, but by then the rain was already upon us, apparently from a large hosepipe rather than a cloud. I've yet to see a more affecting example of the power of nature.

Coincidentally, another storm rolled in on our first evening in Hawnby. Thunder echoed down Bilsdale for half an hour before it

Blue mist, Hawnby hill

arrived, sounding curiously like the boom of a quarry explosion rather than the distinctive vibrating rumble that I'm used to. Then it was upon us and as I ran for cover in the converted barn; a fast-spiralling formation was clearly visible on the leading edge of the stormcloud. It was the closest I've yet been to seeing a tornado, and if I'm honest I'm not sure I'd want to get any nearer. A huge bolt of lightning shook Easterside Hill and quickly the storm was gone.

The following morning I climbed Easterside, as the dew evaporated in the early sunshine. All was long forgotten and peace had returned to the valley.

OVERLEAF Winter sun, Rievaulx Abbey

Endless view, the Vale of York from the Wainstones

Cleveland Way and Roseberry Topping

A walker obligingly waits just long enough for me to take his portrait during summer on Hasty Bank. Just on the odd occasion I feel it necessary to acknowledge the human race in my work. It is almost always to add scale or a focal point to the image, and in this case works both ways, emphasising the sea of heather while drawing the eye towards him. Remove him from the picture and all interest is lost. He was progressing quickly towards the Wainstones, so I was unable to take his name. It is likely that he will never discover his important role in the making of this volume!

Walker, Cleveland Way

Westerdale summer skies

Hutton Beck, Hutton-le-Hole

Plantation Hill, Rosedale Abbey

Young Ralph Cross, Rosedale Head

Workers burn patches of heather at the head of Glaisdale during March 2007, just visible upwind of the flames. Although I approached closer than this I was concerned about melting my walking boots in my haste to take an image. The men were well versed in their task, and the constant wind channelled the smoke neatly down into the valley. The purpose of the controlled burns is to encourage new growth in the heather, which in turn provides better habitats for local wildlife. In recent years, summer droughts have seen rather more unruly fires sparking up on the Moors, and controlled burns have the added benefit of reducing the flammable material that helps them to spread.

Burning heather above Glaisdale

Stepping stones, Egton bridge

Bright water, Mallyan Spout

Nelly Ayre Foss, near Goathland

OVERLEAF Leaf pool, Thomason Foss

I always imagine Mallyan Spout and West Beck as a small corner of Middle Earth transposed onto this one. It must be the seclusion and the feeling that someone with the imagination of Tolkien must have designed these features with natural perfection in mind. Prepare to be disappointed if you are searching for Niagara or Angel Falls, but there's something irresistible about this tiny dribble of a waterfall and the bend of the beck that accompanies it. The imagination can run wild with thoughts of what could lie beyond.

Mallyan Spout and West Beck, Goathland

Ferns, Thomason Foss

Down the hill from Goathland and over the bridge at Beck Hole lies the path to Thomason Foss. It could lead anywhere (some might say it leads nowhere) but after a quarter of a mile or so of trudging through mud, a little glade appears and then the falls. Few places can be better to spend a day in autumn, or indeed any time of year.

Thomason Foss in spate

Eller Beck at Beck Hole

West Beck, Goathland in October

Bend in the river, West Beck

Winter, Goathland Moor

Sunset and snow above Beck Hole

Autumn scene above Littlebeck

Falling Foss in November.
See page 10 for the
description of shooting
this image.

Edge of the Foss

Leaf swirl, Falling Foss

A whirlpool of leaves forms at the bottom of Falling Foss during autumn when the falls are in a relaxed mood. The shoot necessitates a scramble down a muddy bank and up an even muddier beck, plus an extended session of standing in very cold water. All worth it, of course.

Blurred water, May Beck

Warm light, May Beck

Sunlight is rarely helpful when shooting enclosed woodland streams like this one, but there is an exception to every photographic rule. This is another very early effort from the lens of my Fuji G617, and the sort of image that encouraged me to press on regardless of any failures.

South of the bridge, May Beck

Bracken, Biller Howe Slack

The Hole of Horcum in March

The hidden fall, Stevenson's Piece

Fen bogs, Fylingdales

Dusk, Sneaton High Moor

Trees at Helwath Plantation

I rarely combine coastal and inland shoots, but this particular day began at Sandsend and Runswick Bay (images that can be viewed in *The Yorkshire Coast*) and ended with an unplanned stop-off at the top of Blue Bank on the Whitby to Pickering Road. Spectacular rainstorms roamed around all day, and while faint rainbows had been visible on the coast, here one burst out in quite vivid colour. With the sun being so close to the horizon, a ridiculously wide and distorting lens would have been needed to capture the full arc, but those wishing to trace its course to the other pot of gold can find the other end of this giant on the title page of this volume.

Rainstorm from Blue Bank

Winter scene, road to Robin Hood's Bay

Scampston poppies in July

Poppies and sky, above Heslerton

A rare case of hoar frost, or rime (I still struggle with the definitions of the two), in the Vale of Pickering. The problem with shooting it is that the freezing fog that created it must clear to allow for a good image, and then if the sun emerges it quickly begins to fall on top of you, as it did here shortly afterwards!

Winter dawn, Staxton Carrs

Sunset at Langdale End

Spring growth, Raincliffe woods

Bales and cloud, Muston Wold

Blossom, Muston village

Frosted dawn, near Muston

Frozen sunrise, Yorkshire Wolds

Horses in snow, Hunmanby Wold

Like humans, animals rarely make an intentional appearance in my work. I don't have the patience of a dedicated wildlife photographer, but here I waited just long enough for the horses to split and form recognisable 'horse shapes' on the carpet of snow. Above the snowy roofs of Hunmanby the view extends to the hump of Bempton Cliffs – one of the few locations where the Yorkshire Wolds and coast meet.

Dark sun, Wolds

July sunset, Wolds

Unripe wheat, Wolds

Bales and sky, Hunmanby Wolds

Snow shadows, Hunmanby

The Alps? The Highlands? The Sierra Nevada? No, just the Yorkshire Wolds again.

Thunderhead, Hunmanby Wolds

A stunning evening in late summer brought me to an unremarkable field at a Wolds crossroads. The hay bales and lines of course help with composition, but the real story was in the sky. Three separate storm formations vied for my attention, and eventually the passing cloud revealed a dying stormcloud, a few miles out to sea and quickly fading from view. Already being in the right place at the right time, I was able to react quickly to capture it. Being there is the most important factor in landscape photography.

Endless sky, Hunmanby

Windblown rape, Wolds

Sledmere memorial

Harvest time, Butterwick

Treeline and snow, Foxholes

Storm Clouds, Wolds road

It's well over a hundred years since St Martin's in Wharram Percy saw any worshippers, and even then they were 'away fans' from surrounding villages, the village itself having been abandoned in the sixteenth century. The tower was reputedly brought down by a storm in 1959. Despite this neglect and decay, I'm more drawn to it than if it had been perfectly preserved. The silence at dawn is unusual for such a subject, with only moles for company it seems.

Deserted church, Wharram Percy

Evening mist, Thixendale

The essence of the Wolds? It's hard to capture, but at Thixendale, and the nearby Fairydale, I've come as close as I can. Unusually the haze here is not that of dawn but a September evening; it extended all the way from the chalk coast (where it was too thick to shoot) to the chalk hills. The highland cattle at Fairydale (overleaf) add a strange juxtaposition to an already curious landscape. I must admit that I'm not usually shy of skipping over a farmer's fence in the search of a better angle, but those horns have always made me think twice.

OVERLEAF Highland cow, Fairydale

Fairydale chalk quarry, near Thixendale

Quarrying continues on the Wolds in a couple of locations, but mostly what remains are long-abandoned pits. Time heals all wounds, however, and the chalk escarpment created here actually adds to the landscape and shows in a bite-sized chunk what it is made of.

Field lines near Fimber

Evening, Nunburnholme Wold

Late sunlight, Londesborough Park

After sunset, Givendale Hill

Wolds cloudforms in August

Last rays, Givendale

Edge of the Wolds, Cleaving Combe

A single quick recce of Millington Woods in May was enough to tell that the wild garlic had already reached its height, and I found the optimum coverage near the top of the slopes where the trees thin and the path grinds to a abrupt halt. Not paying attention to much else, as usual, the camera bag rolled gently down a slope, crushing the flowers. If there's one thing I didn't want to take home as a souvenir it was the smell, but it followed me around for weeks.

Wild garlic slope, Millington Woods

Waking sheep, near Warter

Winter colours, Warter Village

Iced lake before dawn, North Cave

Bullrush shadows, North Cave Wetlands

All Hallows, Goodmanham

Churches dominate the land on the fringes of the Wolds towards the city of Hull, and many strike remarkable silhouettes against the skyline. St Mary's at South Dalton, with a spire over 60 metres high, is indeed too tall and awkward for me to photograph, though I could perhaps try walking a bit further away! The elegant St Leonard's at Scorborough is wonderfully proportioned and positioned on the edge of the tiny village south of Driffield. I once did a dissertation on the poet Philip Larkin, but never once did I imagine following in his bicycle tracks and 'collecting' churches in the East Riding.

St Leonard's in winter, Scorborough

Warm spring evening, Holme on Spalding Moor

Dragon cloud, Holme on Spalding Moor

Freezing fog, from All Saints Hill, Holme on Spalding Moor

Winter dawn, Holme Hall

The Black Tower, Beverley Westwood

OVERLEAF Beverley Minster, Boxing Day

Beverley Minster took over 200 years to build. Common sense
has prevailed in the intervening years and, but for a few
modern houses poking out of the trees, the view from the
Westwood must have changed little in six centuries. Here, the
sun falls in June, lighting the buttercups and casting dark
shadows on the common land.

Evening, Beverley Westwood

TECHNICAL INFORMATION

All the photographs in this book were taken with a Fuji G617 camera with a 105mm Fujinon lens, excepting the following, which were shot with a Fotoman 617 and the following lenses:

Page 22, White Horse of Kilburn: 180mm Rodenstock lens
Page 37, Plantation Hill, Rosedale Abbey: 180mm Rodenstock lens
Page 42, Nelly Ayre Foss: 90mm Caltar lens
Page 78, Frosted dawn, Muston Wold: 180mm Rodenstock lens
Page 102, Evening, Nunburnholme Wold: 180mm Rodenstock lens
Page 108, Wild garlic slopes, Millington Woods: 180mm Rodenstock lens
Page 111, Waking sheep, near Warter : 180mm Rodenstock lens
Page 120, Black Tower, Beverley Westwood: 180mm Rodenstock lens

Both cameras take four shots per roll on 120 film. A 0.3ND centre filter was used on the Fujinon and Caltar lenses to avoid light fall-off on the edges of the frame. It is essential to use this filter unless a bright circle in the centre of the image is required.

The film used was exclusively Velvia 50 asa.

I recommend the use of Lee Filters for all types of landscape photography. The filters used in this book were:

Neutral density graduated range, including 0.3, 0.45, 0.6, 0.75, and 0.9 strengths. These are generally used to balance the light from the sky with that on the ground and make no colour adjustment to the image.

81 warm-up series including 81B, 81C, 81D and 81EF These are used in low-light situations such as woodland, where the Velvia film's natural inclination towards a blue cast can be unpleasant.

105mm linear polarizer

Although a polarizer must be used sparingly, it can be a very useful tool in bright sunshine to enhance skies and remove reflections from water and foliage. With the panoramic format in particular, care must be taken to avoid the filter causing greater polarization on one side of the image than the other. I will usually take an image with and also without the polarizer in these circumstances.

The light meter used for exposure calculations was a Pentax Digital Spotmeter. This is a beautifully simple and accurate piece of equipment, and supplies EV light readings only, from a 1-degree spot sensor.

The tripod used was a Manfrotto 055Pro.

Processing was carried out by Bob Harvey at NPS Media, Middlesbrough. They have yet to make a single error in processing my film after over 2,000 rolls, not something that can be said about some others I've used for far less work. A small proportion of the images were processed by Positive Images of Richmond, Surrey, and I can also recommend them on the basis of a more limited sample.

All images were scanned using an Imacon Flextight 343 scanner, and colour corrected in Photoshop CS2.

Although most of my recorded exposure readings have unfortunately been lost during the making of this book, I can be contacted for advice, or details of any of the images at markdentonphotographic@yahoo.co.uk. Limited edition prints of the images are also available at www.markdentonphotographic.co.uk

ACKNOWLEDGEMENTS

I'd like to thank all those who helped directly with the making of this book. The support of Joe Cornish and everyone at Joegraphic, in particular Liz Johnston, was, and continues to be, invaluable. Bob, Margaret, Ian, Tina and Peter at NPS Media have given me superb service and the help of Graham Merritt at Lee has been tremendous.

Can I also thank the staff at Frances Lincoln for their tremendous efforts in selling *The Yorkshire Coast* and for their continued support?

I'd also like to thank my friends Anthony Mortimer and Glynis Hunt for moral support, and Paul Brown, David Marshall, Matt and Jackie Hough, the late Dave Sallitt, Pete Leeming and Ben Poussard for logistical help.

Finally, I'd like to thank my family for the fantastic support they have offered me, and accepting my comings and goings, my surprise visits and disappearances!